Souvenirs from the Golden Age of Travel

Harold Darling

Abbeville Press · Publishers · New York

Editor: Walton Rawls
Designer: Renée Khatami
Production Supervisor: Hope Koturo

Library of Congress Cataloging-in-Publication Data

Darling, Harold.
  Bon voyage!: souvenirs from the golden age of travel/
  Harold Darling.
    p. cm.
  ISBN 0-89659-898-5
  1. Travel—History,   I. Title.
G156.D37   1990
910—dc20   89-48384
                      CIP

French Line baggage tag on ribbon from the collection of
Anthony R. Conyers.

CONTENTS

Mankind has an innate compulsion to wander, a desire to explore, a need to uncover the secrets of the other side of the hill— or even those beyond the horizon.

■ Throughout the course of human history, as every direction beckoned, there has been no lack of explorers willing to cross the horizon, to venture into the unknown. Marco Polo, Columbus, Balboa, Magellan, and Sir Francis Drake, among others, devoted (and risked) their lives to satisfy man's curiosity about other lands and peoples. However, by late in the nineteenth century, the possibility of true exploration had very nearly vanished. By then, almost every conceivable place already had been visited.

■ With exploration gone, what remained was travel, which likewise involves journeying, but to well-known (though sometimes distant) places. Traveling often entails struggle, the facing of hardship and danger, yet like explorers of old, who most often kept detailed journals, travelers sometimes recorded and shared their vagabond perceptions of foreign parts through their own writings. Well-known writer-travelers like Sir Richard Burton, Lafcadio Hearn, Henry Adams, D. H. Lawrence, Evelyn Waugh, Richard Halliburton, Freya Stark, and Peter Fleming communicate through their writings a kind of wisdom that strikes a universal chord.

■ Tourism began in the mid-nineteenth century, when entrepreneurs like Thomas Cook conspired to make traveing more desirable to the upper-middle classes by stripping it of the inconvenient and the unfamiliar. The early travel agents wove a network intended to expedite the tourist from distant place to distant place with the ease and predictability of a Londoner's trip by hackney from Whitehall to World's End. Today we rarely have the opportunity to become explorers, but we may choose to be either travelers or tourists. There are few clear-cut distinctions to our choice, but the genuine traveler will pride himself on not being mistaken for a tourist, will eschew the packaged tour, make an effort to see places off the beaten track, actually attempt to communicate with the natives, or residents, and will refuse to swallow the old bromides developed to describe or characterize every country, city, and monument. Instead, the real traveler will seek personal discoveries in every unfamiliar place or custom, for there is little reason why someone cannot make out of the most controlled and unimaginative itinerary a true voyage of discovery.

■ To be a genuine traveler is to launch a process of discovery, to personally reenact the legendary hero's odyssey. This necessitates the separation of oneself from the familiar, the enduring of challenging ordeals, and, finally, the return, altered in many perceptible and imperceptible ways, to one's ordinary life. "It is impossible," the poet W. H. Auden says, "to take a train or an airplane without having a fantasy of oneself as a great hero setting off in search of an enchanted princess or the Water of Life."

■ We who live in a rich and highly developed society also seek in travel an escape from everyday tedium, an improved perspective on our own lives, a little unaccustomed danger, perhaps, but definitely a taste of the exotic.

"But travel is work. Etymologically a traveler is one who suffers travail, a word deriving in its turn from Latin tripalium, a torture instrument consisting of three stakes designed to rack the body."
Paul Fusell
Abroad (1980)

"Englishmen traveling in France noted how rare it was to encounter fellow travelers, much less fellow countrymen. Arthur Young in the late eighteenth century found 'a paucity of travellers that is amazing'; he traveled a whole day on a main road thirty miles outside of Paris and 'met but a single gentleman's carriage, nor anything else on the road that looked like a gentleman.' . . .

"What is travel? All travel, as Freya Stark says, is a quest, a conscious or unconscious searching for something that is lacking in our lives or in ourselves. This it always has been, though in the days before the world became black with ink it was a more conscious quest for more material things. Now that there are no new markets to be found, no new goods to buy, no new lands with unknown riches to discover. . . . The modern traveler travels for himself alone. His reasons for going are purely personal, as are the gains of his travels."
M. A. Michael
Traveller's Quest (1950)

VISITEZ
L'EXTRÊME·ORIENT
PAR LES
MESSAGERIES MARITIMES

For each of us, in truth, there are different golden ages. Sir Richard Burton, who in 1853 was the first nonbeliever to invade the Holy City of Mecca (his life at risk had his disguise failed him), would certainly have been bored by the predictability of luxury liners and grand hotels. He, like other great travelers of the Victorian Age, craved huge helpings of risk and difficulty to make a pungent meal of his voyaging. On the other hand, the would-be traveler of today, like most of humankind, loathes fleas, riding camels dying of thirst, facing bandits with truly murderous intentions, and trying to thaw frostbitten hands over sputtering candles in subzero weather. One likes his comfort and ease, and yet one longs to experience the exotic, walk paths seldom trod, and spy on sacred dancers of Kabir at their secret ancient rites. Alas, these are mutually exclusive desires, for the exotic has a way of evaporating just as the tourists arrive.

''The grand hotel and the railway station, institutions frequently linked in the first half of the nineteenth century, were perhaps the two most striking new building types to emerge in the Victorian era. The development of easy and rapid transport altered people's social expectations, while the accompanying grand hotel also fostered a new detachment from ancient patterns of living. Overnight accommodation in the course of travelling ceased to be a painful necessity and became an occasion to indulge in a fantasy world where travellers could imagine themselves liberated from the responsibilities of the family and the private house. It is this romantic escapism that, in part, accounts for the continuing popular fascination with grand hotels felt even in our own day. The hotel constitutes a kind of theatre in which visitors act out a life that may have little relation to their experience in the real world outside.''

David Watkin
Grand Hotel (1984)

■ The grand hotel simply could not exist off the beaten track, but, nevertheless, by 1880 there were fine, Western-style hotels in many a faraway place. Confidence in finding decent accommodation abroad was partly instrumental in launching what we now recognize as the true Golden Age of Travel, a fabulous era brought to an abrupt halt by the international turmoil of World War I. By this time, all accoutrements for carefree "exploration" of exotic lands were available. Luxurious ocean liners regularly plied the seven seas and passenger trains carried the traveler to almost any destination in first-class splendor. However, the destination hotels might range down the scale from grand luxe to the respectably adequate. Perhaps most significant, the local residents in foreign climes remained in a pleasant state of respectful equilibrium. Although they might find the invading Westerners outlandish, they were prepared to tolerate, even welcome them.

■ The appearance of guidebooks helped to make the journey more rational by providing enough basic information about the not-to-be-missed sights to liberate the traveler from the clutches of the local guide—and the stigma of appearing a tourist. The German firm Baedeker was the first to undertake a program of guidebooks; by 1846 the series was available also in French, and in 1861 it appeared in English. Around the turn of the century, the French tire manufacturer Michelin began its own series of maps and guidebooks. These, and the others, were deeply researched (Karl Baedeker traveled incognito to confirm and update information supplied by his scouts). Altogether, more information than a traveler was ever likely to need was freely available. Finally, travel agencies developed, with the mission of planning every aspect of a voyage, easing any pains a traveler might encounter. And yet, despite the provisioning of all requisite comforts, all of this taming of the experience, there still was left a considerable potential for treading upon truly foreign soil. The limitations on communication were still holding back the inevitable process of world homogenization.

"Never was travel to Europe so pleasant as in the summer of 1914, never before, and never again. Signor Marconi's invention had dispelled the dread mystery of the oceans, and Europe was only five days away. The new superliners were very elegant and far more comfortable than most people's homes. Travel on the Continent was easy and luxurious. The long years of peace had given a spurious air of permanence and progress to the European economy. No passports were needed in that enlightened summer. The hotels and luxury trains like the Simplon-Orient and the Train Bleu were in their heyday."
The History of the American Express Company (1968)

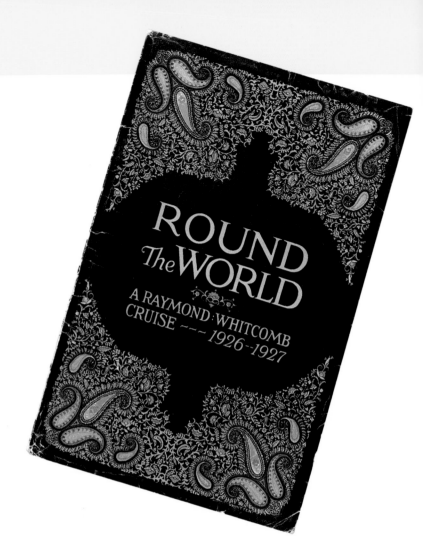

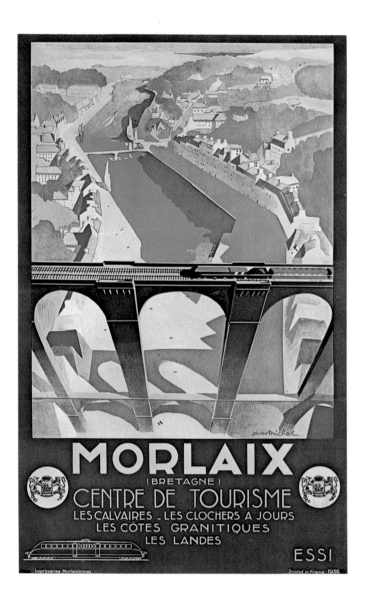

■ It was still a time when Swiss cows wore great bells, and Polynesian maidens, in their daily activities, could be seen wearing grass skirts—and nothing else. The old buildings moldered gracefully, not yet having been spiffed up or heavily rebuilt. In ancient churches and monasteries, friars with large rings of keys led visitors from painting to painting to fresco, perhaps illuminating them by torchlight. Muezzins in their minarets called the faithful to prayer without the aid of electronic amplification. There was still in the heart of foreign places an essential difference, and yet even that could be ignored by some of those who were comfortably transported through hotel gates in the still uncommon automobile and lodged in magnificent settings.

"Half a century ago, well within living memory, international travel, catering overtly for the relatively rich, rare and energetic, was hardly at all like this. Generally, tracks were beaten and paths smooth but the unexpected often happened and, because the speed of advance was not very fast and every scene differed vividly from the last, there was a sense of adventure and discovery in most journeys."
Charles Owen
The Grand Days of Travel (1979)

GRAND-HOTEL KAISERHOF

WIESBADEN

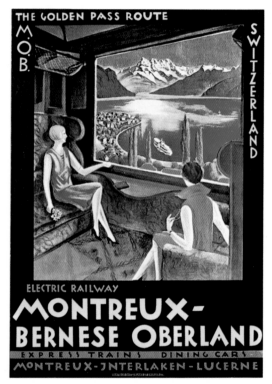

THE GOLDEN PASS ROUTE

M.O.B.

SWITZERLAND

ELECTRIC RAILWAY

MONTREUX–
BERNESE OBERLAND

EXPRESS TRAINS · DINING CARS
MONTREUX · INTERLAKEN · LUCERNE

HOTEL MÉTROPOLE
NICE

''Cook has made travel easy and a pleasure. He will sell you a ticket to any place on the globe, or all the places, and give you all the times you need and much more besides. It provides hotels for you everywhere, if you so desire; and you cannot be overcharged, for the coupons show just how much you must pay. Cook's servants at the great stations will attend to your baggage, get you a cab, tell you how much to pay cabmen and porters, procure guides for you, and horses, donkeys, camels, bicycles, or anything else you want, and make life a comfort and satisfaction to you. Cook is your banker everywhere, and his establishment your shelter when you get caught out in the rain. His clerks will answer all the questions you ask and do it courteously. I recommend your Grace to travel on Cook's tickets; and I do this without embarrassment, for I get no commission. I do not know Cook.''

Mark Twain

A Tramp Abroad (1880)

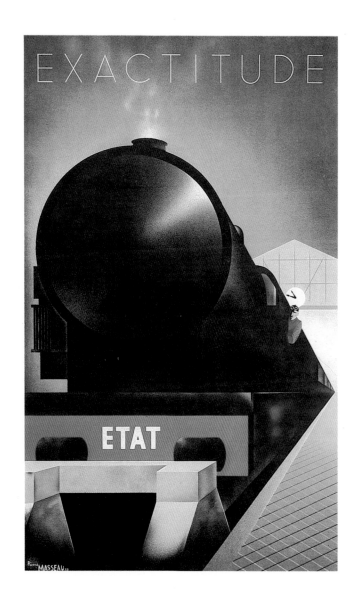

Our idea that certain countries, cities, and sights are more worthy of attention than others has its origins in the English upper-class concept of taking the Grand Tour, which was born in the Renaissance and reached its apogee in the eighteenth century. The notion was that to become a cultured person one needed to visit certain cities, see certain churches and museums, and experience certain views on the Continent. While abroad, it was desirable to study the languages and introduce oneself to the leading citizens of foreign lands. Among the benefits of this tour was the broadening of one's perspective and the stimulation of fresh thinking. Even today, the grand tour lives on in the belief that young people can benefit from a European journey, during or after their college years, before settling down to adult life. Also, the hierarchy of countries and cities implicit in the group tour continues to hold. In the eighteenth century, a proper Englishman's first-choice destinations would be Paris and Rome, and these are still first choices. Thomas Cook and Company, the earliest of great travel agents, helped shape our desires through his suggestions. The various series of guidebooks that began to proliferate late in the nineteenth century also helped us to make choices, particularly through the aid of rating systems sporting multiple dots and stars. With the confluence of all these means for making travel effortless, major tourist centers developed, and in the Golden Age of Travel luxurious accommodations and amenities awaited those who journeyed.

Spain

For the traveler, Spain has always represented sunshine and romance, especially to the resident of the British Isles. For a northerner, Spain's relentless sunlight, reflecting from white walls, was a powerful vision. The country's fusion of European and Moorish traditions made it a place both exotic and accessible. Because of this cultural interplay, cities in the south of Spain (Seville, Granada, Córdoba, and Cádiz), where Moorish influences were everywhere more noticeable, were the principal destinations of tourists in the Golden Age.

France

In the Golden Age, France was the most fully explored country in the world. Paris is still, for many travelers, the city of cities, the goal of goals. Radiating out from Paris, like rays of the sun, are roads and railways that carry visitors to marvelously diverse and fascinating landscapes and towns.

■ The first true foreign "package tours" were arranged by Thomas Cook and Sons in 1862 when the company offered English tourists the opportunity of visiting Paris with all arrangements made and paid for in advance. Since the time of that clever development, the rush of tourists has never ceased. The magnetism of the glamour, sophistication, and sensuality that Paris offers is beyond analysis.

■ Other parts of France were also very popular in this period and included the chateau district along the Seine, Brittany (where people could still be seen in medieval costume even in the 1920s), the Rhône Valley (which exudes the languor and fragrance of the South), Normandy (which boasts magnificent chateaus, dramatic seascapes, and moldering seaports), the Pyrenees (with high mountains for winter sports), and, finally, the French Riviera with its countless enticements.

CARCASSONNE

Hôtel de la Cité

AIX-LES-BAINS

LE PRINTEMPS
EN BRETAGNE

Hôtel de France
St BRIEUC

CHEMINS DE FER DE L'ETAT

EXCURSIONS AU
MONT St MICHEL

Italy

Since the early days of the Grand Tour, Italy has been of central importance to travelers. Most Americans and Europeans sense that treading the stones of this venerable country brings them closest to our Western political and intellectual origins. Greece was surely the greater civilization, but ancient Rome pushed its culture and customs outward over the earth and forward in time. The flowering of art and learning that we call the Italian Renaissance is another powerful draw to the Italian peninsula, for the paintings and buildings of this period have an unmatched appeal to travelers. Finally, the very character of the Italians has always been a strong factor in Italy's popularity, because they of all people, century after century, seem to know best how to enjoy life.

■ Rome was, for the Golden Age traveler, the supreme magnet in all of Italy; however, Florence, Siena, and the other northern city-states with their displays of Renaissance glory were hardly less popular. Venice exerted a powerful appeal because its splendor was less touched by modernity than any other Italian city. It was the discovery and excavation of ancient Pompeii and Herculaneum in the eighteenth century that helped nearby Naples and Capri attract foreign visitors, and their appeal has continued.

HÔTEL SUISSE
ET DES ILES BORROMÉES
BAVENO
LAC MAJEUR·LIGNE DU SIMPLON
MOLTENI ARTI GRAFICHE·MILANO·LUGANO

CAPRI
QUISISANA E
GRAND HOTEL

ALBERGO
MAESTOSO
FIRENZE
STESSE CASE: ALBERGO TERMINUS MILANO
ALBERGO METROPOLI
E. MENGIARDI

HÔTEL
FLORA ROME
SITUATION SPLENDIDE
VIS-A-VIS VILLA BORGHESE
PROPRIETA ARTISTICA
RICHTER & C. NAPOLI
RIPRODUZIONE VIETATA

Switzerland

''Switzerland is unlike anything but itself. Its scenery combines in a remarkable way the wild and the cultivated. The contrasts presented in the wonderful turquoise-colored lakes, neat closely cropped meadows of the valleys, resembling patchwork quilts, with picturesque nestling villages or isolated chalets immaculate in their tidiness, stupendous crags of towering mountains with their background of snow-capped peaks, make a picturesqueness that is individually its own. . . .

■ ''Switzerland is the park-like playground of Europe. Its art and architecture are of no consequence, but in scenery it is preeminent. Its hotels are the best, and most reasonable on the continent, and it makes a specialty of catering to the tourist.''

Edward Hungerford
Planning Your Trip Abroad (1922)

Germany

Despite the bitterness caused by the events of World War I, Germany continued to be a popular tourist destination after the war, for its ancient cities and mountaintop castles had not suffered the fate of France's towns and villages. Rhine voyages were the most popular feature of German travel, for that mighty river is navigable for 525 miles, from Basel in Switzerland down to its North Sea mouth. A journey either on the river or beside it, with numerous lay-bys, was a scenic and cultural feast.

Other European Countries

In 1927 Thomas Cook and Sons offered travelers at least twenty luxury conducted tours of the Continent. Among those tours, eight would take the traveler through one or more of the Low Countries, two included Austria and parts of Czechoslovakia (newly created out of Austrian and Hungarian lands following World War I), and two promised to guide tourists through one or more of the Scandinavian countries. Only one took in Russia on its itinerary.

HOTEL DE L'EUROPE
AMSTERDAM
HOLLAND

ANDORRA-PARK-HOTEL
ANDORRA LA VELLA
(Principat d'Andorra)

Lands of SUNLIT NIGHTS 1938

SWEDEN NORWAY
DENMARK FINLAND

CONTINENTAL PALACE
CONTINENTAL PALACE
CASINO
BLANKENBERGHE BELGIQUE
CREATION EDM GERARD DEVET BRUX

The British Isles

England was particularly fascinating for American travelers since so many of them were acutely conscious of their British heritage. Visitors from the United States were often likely to approach Britain in the spirit of the poor boy returning in maturity to the village of his youth eager to display his wealth and flaunt his accomplishments. Britain exercised myriad attractions. Perhaps foremost, the American tourist could speak and be understood, listen and understand—an experience rather foreign to the innocent abroad. Further, the British way of doing things had a familiar ring, closer to our way than in any other European country. Finally, Britain offered a marvelously compact and various blend of natural beauty and historic monuments.

ANGLETERRE

Bonnington Hotel
LONDON

REVINGTONS HOTEL
GREYMOUTH
WEST COAST N.Z.

THROUGH THE TROSSACHS

L M S L·N·E·R

PRINTED IN GREAT BRITAIN

ONE OF THE **LMS** HOTELS
ARTHUR TOWLE CONTROLLER

Mrs Patricia Moulard

The **CENTRAL HOTEL** GLASGOW

LNER **SCOTLAND** LMS
ITS QUICKER BY RAIL
Full particulars from LNER and LMS Offices and Agencies

''England will always be a delight to the traveler
in that he finds in a comparatively small compass a
whole world thrilling with interest. Historic
remains are in evidence from the early Roman
times, nearly all in excellent preservation. There is
a variety of scenery, strikingly beautiful, and a
wealth of splendid architectural magnificence. One
is struck with the sense of completeness or finish
of everything in England, and it appears that even
the old forests are little changed since earliest
times.''
Edward Hungerford
Planning Your Trip Abroad (1922)

The Far East

Even today, Asia seems vast and incomprehensible. Imagine what it must have seemed like in the Golden Age—country after country teeming with countless hordes of people, cultures and languages almost completely unfamiliar. Anyone who then journeyed to Asia was questing after the mysterious. Because this foreignness was well recognized, and there were greater distances to travel, fewer Westerners visited the Far East than Europe, but, nevertheless, many tourists did come. Those places Britain had touched with empire were the most popular destinations, because Westerners felt safer in them, but Japan and China were too intriguing to be ignored. In some parts of Asia, a traveler could explore for a full day without encountering another English-speaking person; therefore, guided tours were preferred by those who wished to sample the exotic flavors of the East.

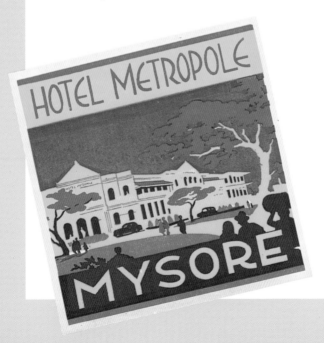

GREAT INDIAN PENINSULARLY.

INDIA FOR THE TOURIST.

"Then, at last, India. I think now that all the countries I had seen before I went ashore at Bombay might be considered as no more than a preparation for this, as though the thirty-four of them had existed only for me as experiences sufficient to give me a sense of proportion with which to understand 'enchanted Hind.' . . .

"I saw much of it, and not many can say more than that, for India is a continent rather than a country and one could spend a lifetime learning to understand a little of one of its areas."
Rupert Croft-Cooke
Seeing the World (1950)

LAURIE'S HOTEL
AGRA
THE HOTZ TRUST, PROPRIETORS.

HOTELS :—
CECIL, DELHI.
CECIL, AGRA.
LAURIE'S, AGRA.
GABLES, MASHOBRA.
WILDFLOWER HALL, MAHASU.

"For me the greatest pleasure is any fresh reminder of the strangeness of the world. As far as travel is concerned, this rules out the Costa Brava, which is like Chelsea on Sunday morning; or Capri, where blue-haired ladies from Minnesota patrol the Piccolo Marina; or even Greece, now that the tourist coaches crowd the road to Delphi. Europe is finished for my kind of traveller. What is left? Fortunately there are the other four continents. If wonders are what you seek, allow me to recommend a journey in Asia: far away and expensive but literally marvellous."

Peter Duval Smith
The Strangeness of Asia (1962)

NIPPON

TOURIST INFORMATION
FOR N. Y. K. PASSENGERS

Actor with mask as young woman in Noh Drama

"It is with the delicious surprise of the first journey through Japanese streets . . . that one first receives the real sensation of being in the Orient, in this Far East so much read of, so long dreamed of, yet, as the eyes bear witness, heretofore all unknown. There is a romance even in the first full consciousness of this rather commonplace fact; but for me this consciousness is transfigured inexpressibly by the divine beauty of the day. There is some charm unutterable in the morning air, cool with the coolness of Japanese spring and wind-waves from the snowy cone of Fuji."
Lafcadio Hearn
Atlantic Monthly (1891)

"About four in the afternoon, you'll be slipping back to the Cathay to change into something long and sleek for tea-dancing at Le Cercle Sportif Français (French Club, for short)—because Shanghai is formal rather than casual at tea-time. And on the way over, perhaps you will be able to wheedle your escort into whisking you, in his long, shining Rolls, through some of Shanghai's crooked, funny little streets; past some of its enticingly reeky markets, where wrinkled yellow merchants offer lacquered ducks as red as cinnabar, sharks' fins that glisten in a drab and jaundiced jelly, drying octopi and eggs that have passed the century mark these many years. Then wend your way through cobbled lanes—thronged and noisy as Piccadilly Circus at midnight on New Year's Eve —where roadside barbers are cropping Chinese pates, and ear-cleaning establishments do a whacking business."
Beatrice Wells (1930s)

ASTOR HOUSE SHANGHAI

北 圓山飯店 台
THE GRAND HOTEL
TAIPEI, TAIWAN

HONG KONG HOTEL

HONG KONG, CHINA

THE IMPERIAL HOTEL
MANAGER
CHÊN YU SHEN
陳玉山 總經理
利通飯店
北平東交民巷滙昌大樓
LEGATION QUARTER (W.ST GATE)
PE PING

GRAND HOTEL DE PEKIN
PEKING

ASTOR HOUSE HOTEL
HONG KONG
MR.
S.S.
FOR

Africa

Africa, the Dark Continent, was in its own way just as mysterious as Asia. It, too, teemed with unfamiliar sights and customs, strange peoples and languages, uncommon dress—or lack thereof. This continent, with the exception of North Africa, was much less explored than Asia. It seemed, whatever the truth, vast and hot and inimical. Only the bold traveler ventured very far from the shores of the Mediterranean. Even by this century, while Thomas Cook and Sons had five offices in Egypt, there were none in the rest of Africa.

"Meanwhile, the crowd ebbs and flows unceasingly. . . . Here are Syrian dragomans in baggy trousers and braided jackets; barefooted Egyptian fellaheen in ragged blue shirts and felt skull-caps, Greeks in absurdly stiff white tunics, like walking penwipers; Persians with high mitre-like caps of dark woven stuff; swarthy Bedouins in flowing garments, creamy white with chocolate stripes a foot wide, and head-shawl of the same bound about the brow with a fillet of twisted camel's hair; Englishmen in palm-leaf hats and knickerbockers, dangling their long legs over almost invisible donkeys, native women of the poorer class, in black veils that leave only the eyes uncovered, and long trailing garments of dark blue and black striped cotton, dervishes in patchwork coats, their matted hair streaming from under fantastic head-dresses; blue-black Abyssinians with incredibly slender, bowed legs, like attenuated ebony balustrades."
Mrs. Amelia B. Edwards
A Thousand Miles Up the Nile (1891)

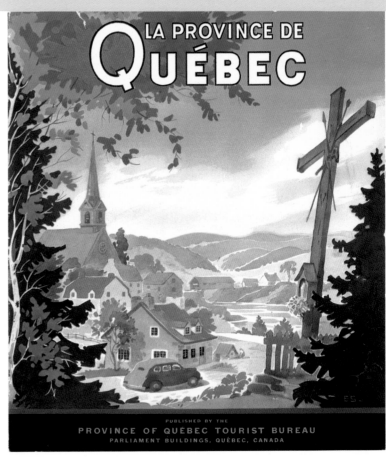

North America

The New World, since the beginning of this period, was a powerful magnet for both the European as well as the American traveler. The European was overwhelmed by the enormous distances to be traversed, in awe of the vastness of the landscape, for in Britain, and on the Continent, most trips could be accomplished in a single day. Many days on the road often separated starting point from destination in America. The Far West provided the European an appealing sense of freshness, a chance to see what the earth must have looked like before the depredations of mankind, for unlike Europe this land had been heavily peopled only decades, not centuries, earlier. Americans, themselves, had the desire to know more of the vast continent it was their "manifest destiny to overspread," to repeat in their own lives their forebears' search for a new life in the West.

"It is of Southern California I am writing. . . . It is a country where the architecture is inclined to fantasy, the flowers and colours to extravagance. Its very landscape has the agitating quality of an El Greco. The tempo of living is slower. One laughs more frequently. Worries fade away, and even the process of thinking becomes lazy and careless.

"After a few months in this strange country, you come magically to slip into the native point of view. Everything in California is so different, and there is always the eternal sunshine which withers old worries and stifles potential new ones. One wakes in the morning filled only with a desire to be out-of-doors."
Louis Bromfield
California (1931)

■ The Eastern Seaboard was not without its natural and man-made attractions, for here were the great cities of Boston, Philadelphia, and New York, the planned splendor of our capital city of Washington, and the wealth of Nature's beauty ranging from the severe charms of rocky and wooded New England to the full tropical radiance of Florida.

THE WASHINGTON MONUMENT AT NIGHT,
WASHINGTON, D. C.

HOTEL
ST·MORITZ
NEW
YORK

108—American Falls from Luna Island, Showing New Rainbow Bridge, Niagara Falls, N. Y.

Latin America

Central and South America were infrequently visited by tourists in the period under consideration. It was not that these areas lacked mythic appeal, but, rather, that one seldom got that far down on one's list of places to visit; then, too, if one did consider going south of the border how would one choose among Uruguay, Peru, Bolivia, Brazil, Guatemala, and Mexico—on and on the exotic and shimmering possibilities offered themselves. Those who did cross the Equator found lands as vast and exotic as in Asia. Only during the 1940s, when the rest of the world was changed by war, did Latin America swim into most people's minds as a glorious destination.

"You are now in Guadalajara City, Jalisco State Capital. It is the economic activities focal point, center of the Mexican Republic occidental coast. It is ubicated 1532 meters over sea level and counts with an annual average climate of 22 degrees. . . .

"His principal symbol, is his catedral- with its qualities towers and as Pepe Guizar (a mexican musical painter borned here) would say in his famous and popular song called Guadalajara: 'Are his Cathedral towers as backstroke plants.'

"Among some attraction places, there is the hospicio cabañas with illustrious mexican artist pictures and frescos. His government palace, where you can still feel history. Over here are murals which are worthy to stop and observe. Its luxurious and traditional Degollado Theater, fun and beautiful expeditions as the Lago-Azul. . . ."
Official Guide to the City of Guadalajara
(c. 1970)

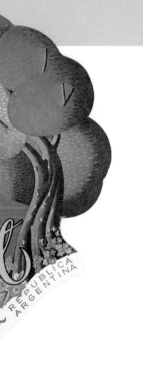

Oceania

"A voyage to the South Seas! The thought summons up visions of beauteous tropic isles where care has never been; bright regions of romance beyond the horizon of a commonplace world.

"And for you who take this voyage, all the romance is to become reality! Your eyes will see the strange volcanic peaks towering high into the blue; you will behold the palm-crested coral isles with glittering white beaches and placid lagoons beyond. You may wander through thickets of banana and breadfruit trees, and feast royally in groves of cocoanut palms. Your soul is destined to be sated with fragrance of hibiscus and frangipani and orange blossoms, with all the wild aromas of the jungle. Though you return to harsher climes, your ears will be haunted with remembrance of the soft ceaseless murmur of the surf upon the reef."

Union Steam Ship Company brochure (1922)

The early history of travel and exploration is, in large part, a chronicle of transportation difficulties. Tales of endlessly jolting carriages, muddy roads, impenetrable fogs, impassable snowbanks, thirsty animals, mired sledges, hostile natives, dust storms, recalcitrant bearers, becalmed or storm-tossed vessels all bear witness that progress across the world has always been difficult, frequently agonizing. But, gradual improvements in roads and means of mobility eventually made travel relatively easy by our era.

■ In the nineteenth century, a travel network was developed by which horse-drawn coaches, railroads, and passenger ships could be so coordinated that a traveler could move from place to place with predictable speed and success. Further, this multifaceted transport could be arranged and paid for in advance so that on the road the traveler was freed of the necessity of dealing with surprise, negotiation, and disappointment.

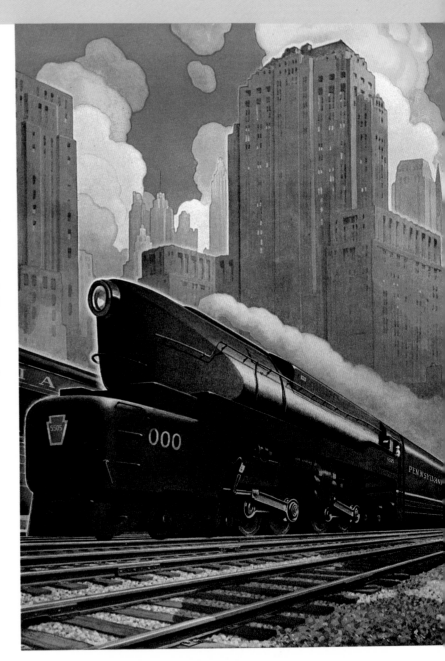

Miss Phoebe Snow
Has stopped to show
Her ticket at
The Gate, you know.
The Guard, polite,
Declares it right.
Of course—
It's Road of
Anthracite.

Lackawanna Railroad

Railway

The first genuine railway journey occurred in 1825. Within fifty years, networks of railroad tracks radiated out of most cities of the world. In 1883 the legendary Orient Express first steamed out of Paris, with compartments featuring easy chairs that converted into beds, stained-glass windows, Turkish carpets, carved woodwork, inlaid furniture, and fine French cuisine in the dining car, as well as an abundance of porters and washrooms. One could travel thus luxuriously from Paris to the Black Sea without changing trains or repacking one's bags. Rail service of this quality so radically changed the standards of transport that its inception can be said to have initiated the Golden Age of Travel.

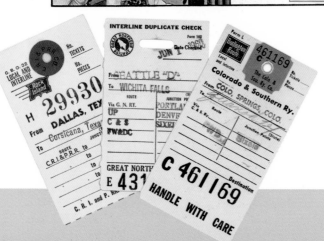

CHICAGO
AND
NorthWestern
SYSTEM

Southern Pacific
Daylight
LOS ANGELES - SAN FRANCISCO

NAME

ADDRESS

CITY

STATE

"Green aisles of Pullman cars
Soothe me like trees
Woven in old tapestries. . . ."
William Rose Benét

Santa Fe
El CAPITAN

H-4582—SANTA FE STREAMLINER ENTERING SOUTHERN CALIFORNIA THROUGH THE ORANGE GROVES

" 'The Chief' is frankly intended for people who
want the best . . . for men who demand the extra
roaming space provided by the club cars and
for women who love daintiness and immaculate
surroundings."
Railway Wonders of the World (1936)

"Here we were on an engine of the most powerful kind in the world, attached to one of the most famous of all travelling hotels—the string of coaches called The Flying Scotsman—with its Cocktail Bar and Beauty Parlours, its dining saloons, decorated in more or less credible imitation of the salons of 18th century France, its waiters and guards and attendants of all sorts, its ventilation and heating apparatus as efficient as those of the Strand Palace Hotel."
Eric Gill
From his letters (c. 1936)

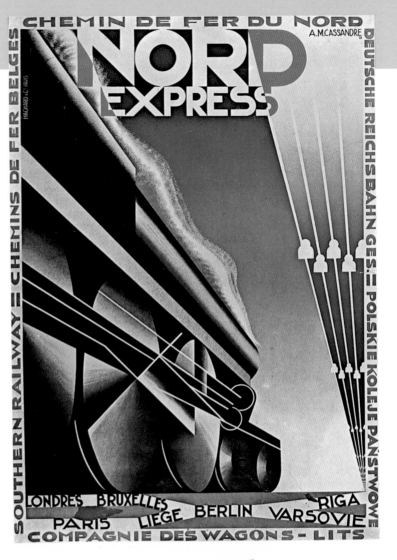

Automobile

Before 1900 the automobile was a rare novelty. After the turn of the century it became increasingly commonplace, and its numbers burgeoned every year, with roads gradually improved to accommodate its increasing speeds. There were great cars available for travelers in the Golden Age: Hispano Suiza, Rolls Royce, Mercedes Benz, Duesenberg, Packard, Stutz, Pierce Arrow, and Daimler. Many other companies also produced luxury cars of unique beauty and workmanship. Auto travel itself could be adventuresome in this pioneering time (frequent flat tires, bumpy roads, and mechanical breakdowns far from garages were common), but the ultimate freedom in mobility exercised a powerful appeal.

"Nothing ever changed so profoundly my material existence, the mechanism and range of my everyday life, as the possession of a motor car."
Leonard Woolf
Diary entry (c. 1945)

"Europe is a veritable paradise for automobile owners, and to cover Europe or part of it en auto is certainly the most delightful, although the most expensive, method of seeing the countries and their peoples. Good roads cross and re-cross the Continent like the strands that bound Gulliver, and good hotels all but rub gables with each other."
Edward Hungerford
Planning a Trip Abroad (1922)

Ocean Liner

Comfortable travel by ocean-going vessel was increasingly common from 1820 onward. Throughout the last decades of the nineteenth century, voyages became quicker and schedules more predictable as steam power replaced sail power. By the 1880s great steamships transported passengers in true elegance. Supreme among them was *The City of Rome,* which many considered the most beautiful liner ever built. Jet black with cream-colored superstructure, the *Rome* boasted lounge walls lined with brocaded silk, floors of parquet, and furniture covered in velvet or leather. The great era of ocean liners had arrived, and from then until the outbreak of World War II, beautiful ship after beautiful ship was launched to pamper the luxury travelers of the world.

NORDDEUTSCHER LLOYD BREMEN

BRITISH INDIA
S.N. C. Lᴛᴅ.
BEIRA
TO
ZANZIBAR
S.S.

.·. **Menu** .·.

GRAPE FRUIT, ORIENTAL

CAVIAR FRAPPÉ

ROYAL GREEN TURTLE —— CREAM MARIE-LOUISE

FILLET OF SOLE, CARMEN
DARNE OF SALMON, CHAMBORD

ASPARAGUS, CALIFORNIAN SAUCE

LARDED FILLET OF BEEF, ALBERT I
BRUSSELS SPROUTS —— BELGIUM ENDIVE
PRINCESS BEANS
—— PARISIAN POTATOES

POULARDE OF BRESSE A LA BROCHE
CHIP POTATOES

SALAD FRANÇAISE

AMBASSADOR PUDDING —— PEACH SULTANE
PETITS FOURS

NESSELRODE ICE CREAM

BARQUETTE AU PARMESAN

DESSERT —— COFFEE

S.S "BELGENLAND"

Saturday, October 20, 1928

■ On the great liners of that period, three-quarters of available passenger space was devoted to First Class, where the imagination of interior designers was given free reign. The *Mauretania* reeked of Edwardian elegance. The *Conte di Savoia* was evocative of ancient Roman luxury. The *France* rivaled the splendor of the court of Louis XIV. The *Normandie* was, for many, the pinnacle, with its streamlined sleekness and art deco interiors.

■ Whatever line one selected, a ship was available that could be called a work of art. If one could afford the fare, one would be borne across oceans as if the resident of a grand hotel.

"Was it the size of her, that great cliff of upper-works bearing down upon him? Was it her majesty, the manifest fitness of her to rule the waves? I think what brought the lump to the boy's throat was just her beauty, by which I mean her fitness in every way; for this was a vessel at once large and gracious, elegant and manifestly efficient. That men could fashion such a thing by their hands out of metal and wood was a happy realization. Ships he had seen by the hundred thousand, but this was a ship in a million; and there came to him then as he saw her, glorious in the evening sunlight, the joy of the knowledge that this was what his own kindred could do, this was what the men of his own race, labouring on the banks of his own familiar River, were granted by Providence the privilege to create. In that moment he knew that he had witnessed a triumph of achievement such as no God of battles or panoplied monarch had ever brought about."

George Blake,
remembering the just-launched *Lusitania*
Down to the Sea (1937)

''The supreme ecstasy of the modern world.''
Thomas Wolfe, on travel aboard
one of the great liners

GREAT WHITE FLEET
Caribbean Cruises

WHEN you plan to cruise south-ward this winter, think of the romance and history that clusters round every port of call in the Golden Caribbean.

... and your memories of the past are made more enjoyable by the luxurious comforts of the present. For Great White Fleet ships are built especially for tropical cruising. Every room is an outside room open to views of sea and sky; food served is equal in variety and quality to that served in any first-class hotel.

... and there is a fine degree of personal service that makes good the slogan of the Great White Fleet—"Every Passenger a Guest."

Sailings from New York and New Orleans twice every week in the year
Great White Fleet Cruises to the Caribbean carry only first-class passengers and every detail for their comfort and amusement— hotel accommodations, motor trips ashore, railroad journeys, sight-seeing jaunts are all carefully planned in advance—and everything is included in the price you pay for your ticket.

Address Passenger Department
United Fruit Company
Room 1635
17 Battery Place, New York City

Wire for beautiful booklet "Carib-bean Cruises" and leaflets giving full details of Winter Cruises to the Caribbean.

10 to 24-Day Cruises to

Cuba — Havana | Jamaica — Port Antonio, Kingston | Panama Canal Zone — Cristobal | Costa Rica — Port Limon | Colombia — Cartagena, Puerto Colombia, Santa Marta | Guatemala — Puerto Barrios, Guatemala City | British Honduras — Belize | Spanish Honduras — Puerto Cortez, Puerto Castilla, Tela

F. L. King

"Each day we turn the clocks back one hour. Soon we forget time and date completely. The days and nights flow into one another like the waters beneath us. One breathes the air, spicier than Mexico, one touches the sea spray, and floats on the dream of this perfect voyage."
Bertrand de Jouvenel (1935)

"Now, however rich you are, you will never know the frisson of walking up the gangplank of a truly great liner and entering a mirrored labyrinth where ingenuity and flamboyance created a gently rolling world of mystery and sudden splendour out of a metal hulk. Goodbye to all that."
Nicky Bird
*Luggage Labels from
the Great Age of Shipping* (1985)

.THAYAHT. 22

Airplane

At the conclusion of World War I, suddenly unemployed military pilots got the notion of capitalizing on their rare and hard-earned skills by establishing businesses that would transport urgently needed parcels by air. Eventually that service led to the carrying of passengers, and the first successful venture operated between London and Paris. By the early 1920s it was possible to fly from one European city to another, though it was a rather expensive mode of travel. As early as 1909 Germany had offered scheduled flights by dirigible to cities all over Europe, and in 1928 the *Graf Zeppelin* first crossed the Atlantic. In 1935 Pan American's *China Clipper* flying boat initiated flights from the United States to the Far East. Although air flight represented but a small part of travel in the Golden Age, foundations were laid that would, after World War II, make flying the dominant force in world travel.

"The hotel idea is as old as man on the move. The ancient traveller who rigged up a primitive tent and lit a fire for warmth and cooking and to keep the more treacherous fauna at bay was dealing with the essence of the matter on a do-it-yourself basis. His needs were shelter and safety: a place to stop, eat and sleep.

■ "The notion of somebody else providing these facilities for payment followed naturally. The biblical inn was at first an enclosed courtyard and then a public building for the Asiatic wayfarer. The Persians called a group of travellers a karwan, or caravan, and in the same language sarai was a big house; simple addition provides our word caravanserai, which Webster still gives as a synonym for hotel.

■ "By the Middle Ages the travellers' rest was recognisably an hotel, with 'a sign, a host, a staff of servants, a table d'hôte meal and a reckoning.' Comfort and hygiene came earlier into the picture than might be expected, for by 1577 the Reverend William Harrison was writing in his Description of England of 'sumptuous innes . . . very well furnished with naperie. . . . Each commer is due to lie in cleane sheets wherein no man hath beene lodged since they came from the laundresse.' "
Stephen Watts
The Ritz (1963)

Transit Hotel

The hotel developed from a common need: wayfarers away from home required a roof under which to be sheltered and fed at nightfall. Those who lived along well-traveled trade routes were so often petitioned for a night's lodging that some decided to make a business of their hospitality. Thus was born the inn or early hotel.

■ The simplest form of hotel is known as the transit hotel. Most people who must stop in transit settle for the closest and cheapest place to stay. All a transit hotel really needs for success is simplicity, cleanliness, and efficiency in catering principally to business people who often check in late and check out early. Close to the primitive inn in their function, transit hotels account for more lodgers than all the other kinds of hotels combined. While they may put on airs, it is only halfheartedly, for these hotels really are as dull, and as necessary, as kitchen matches or motor oil. It is only a step further to the motel, the natural descendant of the transit hotel.

Vacation Hotel

Since before Roman times, pleasure resorts have grown up near natural springs whose water was commonly alleged to possess health-giving properties. While at first people came to bathe in the springs to improve their health, as time went on this healthful pursuit seemed naturally to lead to the pursuit of pleasure. The English spa Bath became the showplace of elegance, where fancy dress balls, endless entertaining, card playing, dancing, promenades, fireworks, and concerts all flourished. The sea and bathing in it offered the same rationale of self-improvement as the health-giving spring, and seaside resorts such as Brighton and Scarborough grew to be the vacation goals of the lower and middle classes. In France the Riviera with its sunlight played the role of health resort, and Nice, Cannes, and Monte Carlo offered the entertainments. In Germany, Baden-Baden, Marienbad, and Karlsbad grew into resorts where society bloomed, danced, and gambled; the baths themselves becoming a subordinate draw.

Hotels were an obvious necessity at these lush retreats, and they were provided early and in profusion. Some were grand and some were humble, but the full vacation experience tended to call for certain common characteristics. Vacation hotels are homes away from home, and people stay at them for weeks, often returning year after year. The impersonality of the transit hotel or the elaborate facade of the city hotel would be out of place at a resort. The surroundings must seem homey. Even grand hotels in spa locales, like the Brenner's Park Hotel in Baden-Baden, achieve their excellence by ultimate hospitality and quiet rather than by pomp and sumptuousness. People on vacation, more than at any other time, want to be known and welcomed. They need a staff that cares about their comfort. They want to stay in a home like their own—but better. The best vacation hotels achieve this.

PARC PALACE HOTEL GRASSE

VICHY HOTEL DES THERMES

CALDAS DA RAINHA TERMAS HOTEL CENTRAL

Montecatini Terme GRAND HOTEL CROCE DI MALTA

"The spa which had existed in Western Europe since Roman times (and earlier than that in Gaul) centred on a spring whose waters were considered to have health-giving properties. Bath itself was the Roman Aquae Sulis revived; such French spas as Vichy and Aix-les-Bains also dated back to Roman times. By the second half of the eighteenth century the purely curative aspects of these resorts were largely eclipsed by their social and fashionable aspects."

Louis Turner and John Ash
The Golden Hordes (1976)

"The kind of felicity to which the Blue Train conveyed you as it let you off at Marseilles or Toulon or Cannes or Nice or Monte Carlo, whence you could go on to the Italian Riviera, to Rapallo and all the way down to the Amalfi Coast, seemed novel in the 20's. It seems novel no longer because those places have provided the model for the décor and atmosphere of successful international tourism ever since. . . . Wherever exported and transplanted out of Europe—to Turkey, Mexico, even the U.S.S.R.—the style is the same, involving beach and sun, bright colored aperitifs at little tables outdoors, copious fish and shellfish to eat, folk- or popular music played on string instruments, cheap drinkable local wine, much use of oil (olive for cooking, suntan for browning), all in a setting of colored architecture and 'colorful' street markets. A maximum exposure of flesh guarantees a constant erotic undertone, and a certain amount of noise (Vespas, children shouting on the beach) provides a reassurance of life and gaiety."

Paul Fussell
Abroad (1980)

"To a thoughtful mind, remarked the Brighthelm-stone Ambulator *in the eighteenth century, the ocean is always an interesting object; and never did this journal print a truer word. So much salt water all together in a vast expanse, beating or lapping on the edges of the land—no wonder it has always excited the minds, both thoughtful and thoughtless, of mankind. After all, we lived and breathed in it once, more million years ago than we care to count; it is our aboriginal home. Now it seems strange, fantastic, intimidating, alluring, a magical element, a romantic adventure. We leave, when we can, the prose and comfort of cities, brave the turbulent anguish of trains, in order to spend a week, a weekend, a month, beside this chill and romantic waste of waters sliding and tossing up and down delightful shining sands."*

Rose Macaulay
Personal Pleasures (1936)

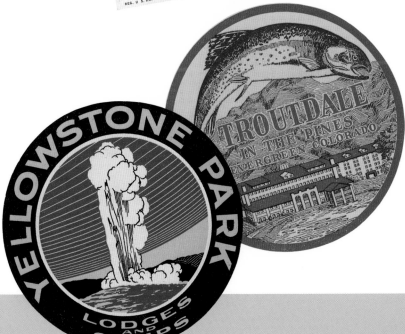

"You can't be comfortable at home and it is useless to try.

"To be comfortable you must go where comfort is—California.

"In California—even in midwinter—wraps and overcoats are unnecessary. The sun shines bright and clear, and there is just enough 'snap' in the air to make it invigorating; just enough warmth to tempt you to spend all day and every day out-of-doors.

"In California—even in midwinter—you can hunt, bathe and play golf. You can catch the biggest fish ever snared by hook and line. You can pick flowers, climb mountains, go a-picnicking, or stroll through the prettiest valleys in America: palms and orange groves all about you and the bluest of blue skies above you."

1903 advertisement

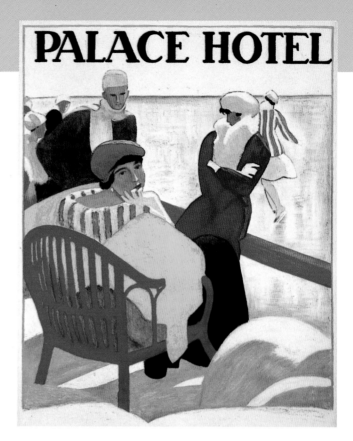

Grand Hotel

The grand hotel, of which there are perhaps only one hundred fifty in the entire world, approaches the ideal. It is not enough that it be luxuriously constructed and appointed. Nor is it sufficient that it employs a large well-trained and temperamentally correct staff. These basic attributes are only the beginning. If a fine hotel can, from generation to generation, offer luxurious appointments, fine food, and superb service, then there is the possibility that someday a subtle alchemy will transform it into a grand hotel. Few hotels survive long enough for this to occur naturally, but even the survivors may fail to attain the magic, may never be so transformed.

■ It sometimes also happens that a certain spirit can forsake a once-great hotel, yet the abandoned shell goes on overcharging and disappointing generations who presume they are checking into an aristocrat among hostelries. There are, to be sure, grand hotels that die in body as well as soul, and many travelers grieve over their passing as long as memory remains.

■ There are hotels that in their youth shine like the stars. But despite this admirable quality, they cannot be said to be grand, for true grandeur requires decade after decade of excellence. This layering of generational memory achieves for a hotel a lustrous quality, a finish with a deep, complex beauty.

■ No matter how superb the athletic skills, how great the accomplishments of a young baseball player, he cannot achieve the Hall of Fame until season after season of excellent play reveals the scope and permanence of his character. So it is with the grand hotel.

■ When we think hotel, most of us think grand hotel (even though few of us have ever checked into one), despite the fact that other levels of hotel outnumber them a thousand to one. This is because the grand hotel approaches as near to the Platonic ideal as is possible. So it is that when we think apple we conceive a shapeliness, crispness, and flavor that we will seldom encounter. We dream ideals as we move among imperfection.

PALACE HOTEL
BRUXELLES

HÔTEL Astoria
BRUXELLES

HOTEL ESPLANADE
BERLIN

LE PLUS BEL HÔTEL DU MONDE
ROYAL PICARDY
LE TOUQUET

BADISCHER HOF
BADEN BADEN

"There is something intoxicatingly theatrical about the best of these places which can transform the dowdiest duckling into a swan. Stage fright, sometimes induced by stuffy, snobbish, and second-rate establishments, should not rear its head at palace hotels, the greatest of which have always generated an unobtrusively friendly and welcoming atmosphere. The tone is set from the start with the smooth removal of luggage, the minimum of fuss over registration at the reception desk, and, above all, the immediate sense of belonging. The guest may be flattering himself, but he feels at home in this fantasy world—and he is encouraged to do so."

Hugh Montgomery-Massingberd
Grand Hotel (1984)

"Take the sort of people who travel constantly around the world. For them, a great hotel is the one where they are best known, where the hall porter calls them by name as they walk through the front door and the assistant manager shows them up to the same room they have always had; and where the housekeeper, as well as arranging the furniture the way they like it, has remembered their wife has a weakness for blue flowers."
Christopher Matthew
A Different World (1976)

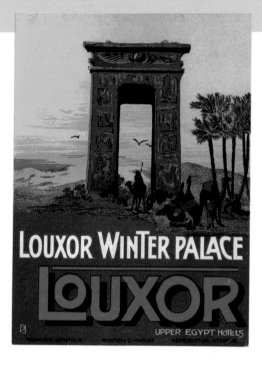

"Hardly have you pulled up at the door when you are swept along by the trappings of this flamboyant realm. A giant in a doorman's uniform opens the door of your automobile and, if necessary, protects you from the rain with an outsized red umbrella, thereby ushering you into that holy of holies, the main lobby. The place is lit up by a blaze of glittering lights, and you could hear a pin drop. A grand hotel's main lobby could scarcely be more antithetical to that of a railway station. Whereas the latter fairly vibrates with the hustle and bustle of people on their way somewhere, the former radiates the calm of people who have arrived and thus live in hushed composure."

Jean d'Ormesson
Grand Hotel (1984)

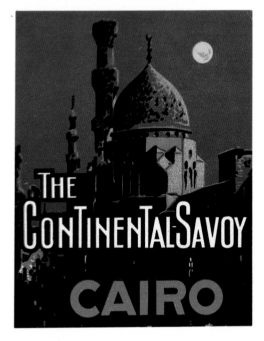

''The one thing I do not want from a hotel is that it should feel like home. There are those who reproduce the feeling all too accurately. There is a rim round the bath and the soap has nearly run out. The sheets are changed only once a week and there are this morning's crumbs in the bed. A light bulb needs replacing in the passage.''
Quentin Crewe (c. 1975)

*"On his second visit he will be left in no doubt
that his is a familiar face. What distinguishes the
great palace hotels from other equally (or often
even more) expensive hotels is not only the noble
proportions of the architecture, the beauty of the
interior decoration, the unsparing quality of the
fittings, and the staff's unfailing personal attention
to detail, but also that elusive commodity—style."*
Hugh Montgomery-Massingberd
Grand Hotel (1984)

■ Grand hotels are those hotels that have achieved near perfection in ambience, setting, and service. They must be beautiful in their architecture and furnishings. They must be large enough to inspire awe, and contain mystery. They must have employees so numerous and well-trained that needs are anticipated and invisibly fulfilled. They must have space, silence, and charm. We all dream of palaces, dazzling bathrooms, perfect sleep in the arms of silence, servants as faultless as genies. A grand hotel is as near as we shall come to experiencing this dream.

Containers for the transport of personal possessions are as necessary and ancient as travel itself. Packs, bundles, handled baskets, saddlebags, chests, and so on, all have been put to use.

■ In the Golden Age of Travel, luggage was more sophisticated, varied, and prodigal. Elegant leather and brassbound trunks, with many drawers and compartments, were the foundation of a traveler's baggage repertoire. People carried with them many changes of clothing, and a full range of costume from sportswear to formal attire, as well as matching footwear and headgear. Often a dozen trunks were taken on a journey, in addition to lots of smaller bags such as vanity cases that contained a great variety of powders, scents, soaps, and a full range of implements—scissors, clippers, buffers, tweezers, and hair curlers. In this era labor was inexpensive, so well-to-do travelers felt no constraints on number, bulk, or weight of baggage.

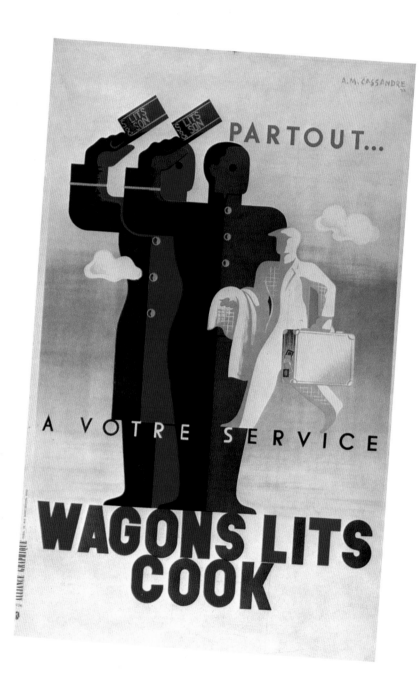

HOTEL GREAT CENTRAL LONDON

"The most conveniently placed and perfectly appointed Hotel in London"—A.L.

GRANDES HOTELES WASHINGTON Y 7 SUELOS GRANADA ALHAMBRA

·HÔTEL·PENSION·
GENÈVE
6-8, Rue du Mont-Blanc
MINERVA

HOTEL DE CASTILLE
ET
St-ANDRÉ
30, Rue Masséna
NICE

HÔTEL LONDRES ET CONTINENTAL
LONDRES GENOVA
GENOVA
TIP. PAPINI

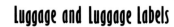

QUEEN'S HOTEL
Gibraltar

HOTEL CONTINENTAL
PLZEŇ
ČSR

*"Tags and labels for baggage may be procured
from the steamship company at the time the ticket
is issued. These bear a large initial, according to
the passenger's last name, and space in which to
write your full name and the number of your
stateroom, name of steamship and sailing date.
Some are marked 'For the Hold,' and others,
'Wanted.' Paste one of the former on each end of
every piece of baggage not wanted in the stateroom, and tie a tag marked "Wanted" on each
piece of baggage that may be needed during the
voyage. Baggage for the hold of the ship should
be sent so as to reach the dock at least a day
before sailing. It will be found there when you
arrive, and when claimed, the baggage master of
the line will see that it is placed on board. Stateroom baggage—steamer trunk, suit case, roll of
rugs, etc.—should accompany the passenger to
the dock the day of sailing, and stewards will
immediately take charge of it and place it in the
stateroom as marked on the tags."*
Edward Hungerford
Planning Your Trip Abroad (1922)

sorry to leave the and →

MIRAMAR
HOTEL
MADEIRA
the Island of Sunshine
and Flowers

with Mr.....................
Travelling .... Class in Cabin Nº.........
By.............................
To.............................

But I be............
if I don't come
back again!

■ Keeping track of all the baggage was a challenge met by tags and labels that alerted handlers to which liner, which cabin, and ultimately which destination hotel a particular valise was to go. These were all distributed to the traveler well before departure. As one's itinerary progressed, more labels were added to the luggage, a record of one's taste (and solvency) in selecting accommodations.

■ A luggage label is a considerable design challenge. It offers only a small area for words that must be clearly read from a distance. Early labels dealt with this through simplicity—a colored background with large letters—but as time went on it became apparent to hotels or transportation companies that issued them that something further was available, namely, self-promotion. This called for an evocation of the hotel's character, which could be accomplished through the correct choice of colors, the right picture, a proper style of lettering, and the overall impact of the design. The more luxurious the hotel and the more its appeal depended on conveying a special ambience, the greater the importance of the label, the more critical the success of its design.

ROYAL GASCOGNE BORDEAUX
GARAGE DANS L'HOTEL

HOTEL NORTE
REVERTITO E HIJOS
Pº FLORIDA, 1
MADRID

HOTEL POULARD
MONT ST MICHEL (MANCHE)
TELEPH. Nº 1
RAY. LE NU

The ROWE
Michigan's Best Known Hotel
GRAND RAPIDS · MICHIGAN
THE FURNITURE CAPITAL OF AMERICA

■ Whatever its form, the luggage label had considerable significance to the Golden Age traveler. A single label might mean very little, but an accumulation testified to the mobility and taste of the luggage's owner. The appeal was not unlike that of rows of ribbons on the military veteran's chest—boastful tokens of glories experienced and travails overcome.

Acknowledgments

We are grateful to the following publishers for permission to include short excerpts from books they originally published: Macmillan Publishing Company; W. W. Norton and Company; Oxford University Press; St. Martin's Press; T. & T. Clark; Vendome Press; the Victoria and Albert Museum; and Webb and Bower.